RAW THOUGHTS

A MINDFUL FUSION OF POETIC AND PHOTOGRAPHIC ART

RAW THOUGHTS
A MINDFUL FUSION OF POETIC AND PHOTOGRAPHIC ART

JOHN CASEY

OTHER BOOKS IN THIS SERIES

MERIDIAN: A RAW THOUGHTS BOOK

PHiR Publishing
San Antonio, TX

Copyright © 2020 by John Casey
Photography © 2020 by Scott Hussey

PHiR Publishing
San Antonio, TX
phirpublishing.com

Second Edition: April 2021

All rights reserved. No part of this book may be reproduced without permission. If you would like to use material from the book (other than for review purposes), please contact permissions@phirpublishing.com.

ISBN 978-1-7370627-1-4
LCCN 2021905945

Printed in the United States of America

For You

raw | ˈrȯ | adjective: not having undergone processes of preparing, dressing, finishing, refining, or manufacture

thought | ˈthȯt | noun: meditation, contemplation, or recollection

THOUGHTS

Foreword — 13
Reflection — 14
Wondering if — 16
Loss — 16
Empty Skies — 18
Stellar — 18
Subsistence of Loss — 20
Skeletons — 22
No One but Me — 24
Missing — 26
Leaving Nothing — 26
Nothing Left and Nothing Right — 28
A Little Emptier — 30
Insanity — 32
Unicorn — 34
Hell — 36
Among the Ashes — 38
A Place for Hope — 40
Walls — 42
Fear — 44
It Just Bleeds — 46
Gossamer — 47

Sweet Nothings	48
Vampire	50
Tempted	50
Amoral	52
Rot in Camouflage	53
Perdition	54
Unfulfilled	56
Apathy	58
As It Seems	59
All Figured Out	60
Carnation	62
Blue	63
Cattle	64
Narcissism	66
Win	66
Would That I Were	68
Evanescence	69
Chasing the Sun	70
Stigma	72
Really?	74
Sloth	74
Stupid	76
The Insanity of It All	76
Quiet	78

Listen	78
Final Act	80
Optimism	82
Honey	84
Gaia	84
Alive	86
In the Ascent	88
Real	90
True Love	92
We Were There	94
With You	94
Sinfonietta	96
Love Song	97
Note from the Heart	98
Flight	100
Ever	102
Pieces of Me	104
Beauty's Smile	106
Little Bunny	107
Gratitude	108
Φ	111
Acknowledgements	112
First Publications	115
About the Author	116

Foreword

"All that we are is the result of what we have thought. It is founded on our thoughts, it is made up of our thoughts."

The *Dhammapada* is the best known and most widely read Buddhist book of scripture. This verse from its first chapter is a metaphysical notion of existence that is a level or two deeper than the average person will typically contemplate. If we allow for the possibility that these words of the Buddha are true, we begin to question the accuracy of our understanding of self. Most tend to believe that what one does and says, how one acts and reacts, is the best measurement of persona. The Buddha expresses here that what and how we think are at the root of all else and implies that much of what is thought results in nothing that is outwardly observable. Thus, we tend to judge these things incorrectly.

We cannot know someone from his or her actions and words alone; we need to understand their thinking. We must learn about them over time and remain empathetic without making assumptions about what we see and hear. Even before we can hope to do this well, however, there is a precondition that we understand ourselves—to examine, understand, and to improve our own thinking, day by day. *Raw Thoughts* helps us accomplish this.

Raw Thoughts is comprised of voyeuristic glimpses of the heart and mind that together chart a path from loss and despair to catharsis, introspection to illumination, and from there to happiness and love. Poetry and photography are combined within to form emotional and provocative vignettes (*raw thoughts*) that exhibit what happens in life with the aim of evoking sentiment and reflection—mindfulness about what can be done to make things better.

At some point you may find yourself on a page that generally represents where you are in life. By then you will have been exposed to where you can go with spiritual regression, and in reading further, where you can evolve by carefully examining, assessing and adjusting how and what you think. You may wonder as well, *"is there a story here?"* In this respect, the book is intentionally vague and open to interpretation. Determine this independently.

If you've lost everything, find yourself.
If you haven't, find yourself anyway. Look inside.

Reflection

So difficult not to stare.
He doesn't deserve to be acknowledged,
but I can't help it.
When I see him, I think about the wreckage he's left behind.
And I think about
everyone he's hurt along the way.
He's taken destruction to a new level.
The only thing he's managed to refine in life is his duplicity.
We'd be better off without him.
It should end.
But somehow, death would be too kind

He sees me looking

                          Staring back purposefully with those judging eyes.
                                 Suddenly, I want to strike him.
                            He needs to be punished for all of it.
                                       I scream at him,
                            but he screams as well, startling me
and I punch him in the face with all my strength, furious.
                             He hits me back with equivalent anger.
                                 I stagger, overcome and crying.
                                Blood drips to the bathroom floor
                                   and I slump down on the toilet
                                         to think some more,
                    picking splinters of glass from my hand

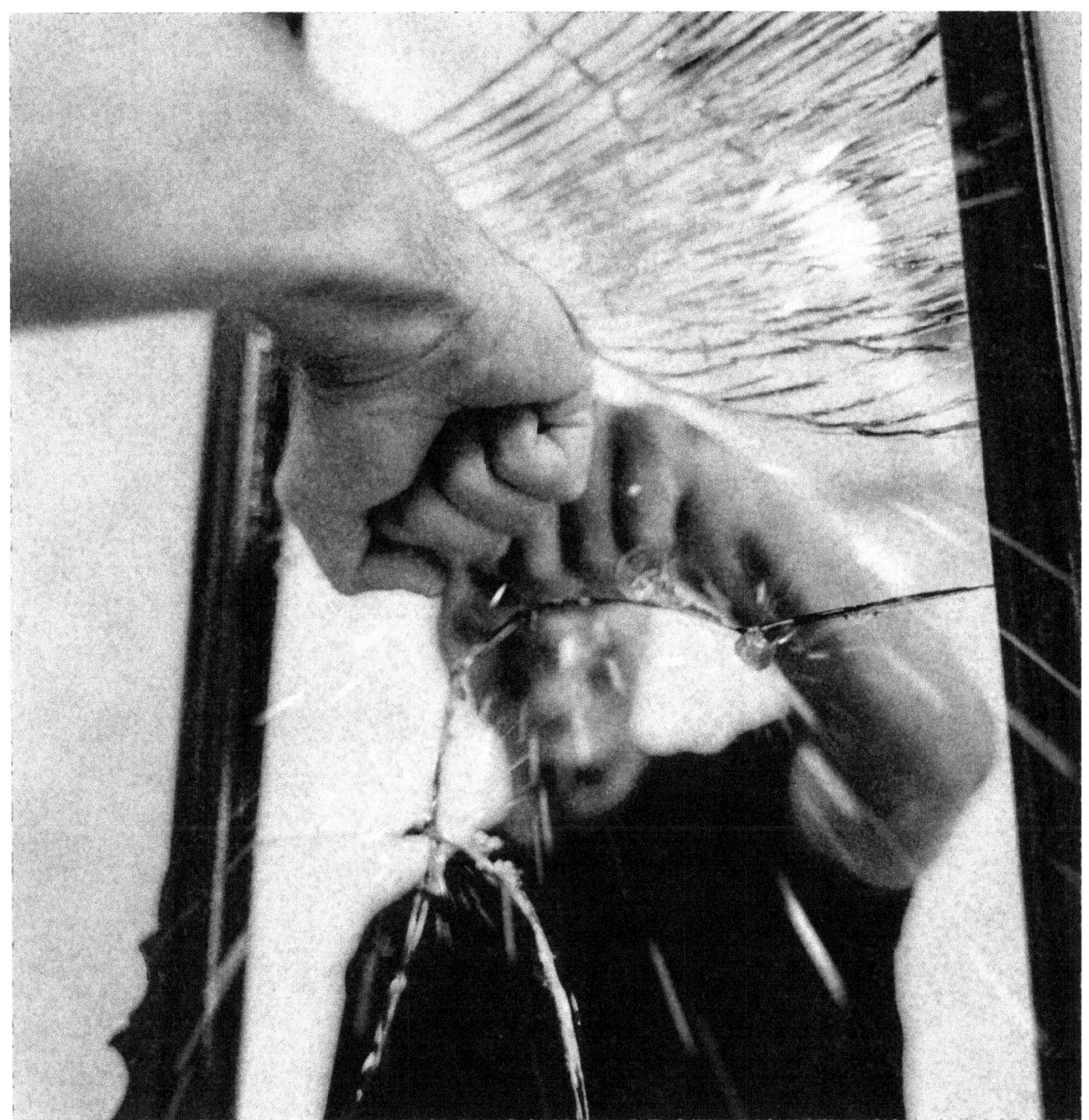

Wondering If

A foreboding, poison sorrow
has settled in my core.
The irony, I cannot tell
what I'm afraid of more

That I may learn what I dread most
insidious, transpired,
or never knowing, wondering if,
unsound, beset and tired

Loss

No chance that I could cope
with life at any cost.
There is no hope for hope,
all I hold dear is lost

The anguish so profound,
dearth in my heart so black.
I leave without a sound
and will never come back

Empty Skies

Where a distant flicker somehow marks the infinite reach of solitude.
Where a deep, silent nothingness whispers lies about fading conceptions of hope,
and the vast, enveloping black delivers an invitation to fear

So easy comes despair.
So easily to tears

Look closer, nearby, and touch wherever tears fall.
Where ethereal is real.
Leave others more qualified to worry for the stars

Stellar

Fleeting feelings cast in space,
contrails of my soul.
Drifting nowhere, out of place,
all as black as coal

Longing for a place to be,
Earth, the Moon, or Mars.
Lost in the periphery,
wishing on the stars

Subsistence of Loss

Better to have loved and lost...
So it is true and yet, in this exists so much sorrow.
A sorrow that fades with time, they say.
But *they*—they are wrong.
Yes, the memories fade.
The details, the colors, tastes, sounds and moments
deliquesce, as air in the vacuum of space.
But the vast, attendant nothing fills inexorably with heartache.
A sorrow that endures

They—they never knew love.
Or, they never lost.
Where the rarified air of true love persists.
It is there, beyond breath,
yet preserved in the cold constancy of sadness

The need to breathe—
air, so intrinsic to life.
So is love the sole averment
of ever having been truly alive.
To have known love and lost
leaves one disconsolate and voided,
forever seeking some course of revival.
A way to bring it back.
To breathe again

Skeletons

We keep them, but we don't really want to.
Most of them don't stay kept for very long.
The good ones, the happy secrets,
come out almost straight away

The bad ones, the deep, dark secrets,
stay hidden the longest.
Festering. Roiling.
Gnawing

But even with these, as terrible as they are,
your desire to be rid of them
continually tests the strength of your resolve
to keep them buried

For instance, I have a secret
I don't want anyone to know about.
I'm afraid of what may happen
If you were to learn of it

I also know that if I were to tell you,
I'd be far better off.
After a time, maybe even happy.
But not today

No One but Me

The wonderful place where my companions,
confidants, and loved ones used to be
has been reduced to baneful ash
by a torrid chain of events.
A careless, buffeting wind
tosses the pestilent soot to and fro,
then upwards, where it hangs in empty space.
Obscuring the horizon,
a wretched haze in every direction

Breathe it in, deeply.
Embrace anguish.
Validate despair

I blame them for leaving
when I needed them most.
I condemn the world for this inhumane existence
that leaves me asphyxiating
on the charred remains of my life.
I will never trust again.
I will never love again.
There is no one left.
No one but *Me*

Missing

Something is missing, I'm not feeling myself,
like I left my soul on a shelf

There's an aching void where my heart used to be
and all that's left is half of me

It leaves me searching to fill this darkened space.
But all I see is your sweet face

Something is missing, flew away like a dove
with my heart, and all that I love

Leaving Nothing

Shadows dance and gather round,
colors fade to black and white.
Silence takes the place of sound,
love drifts slowly out of sight

Dream state pictures fill my mind,
vague, pale echoes of her kiss.
Swirling mists converge, unwind,
leaving nothing. Emptiness

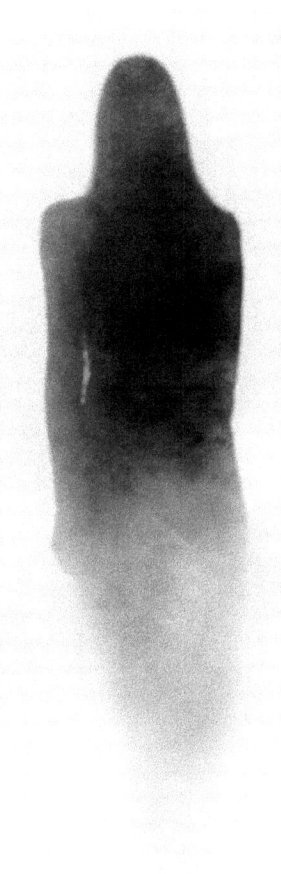

Nothing Left and Nothing Right

Paranoia and mounting chagrin,
adrift in a world of dejection.
Reality begins to set in,
I have lost all sense of direction

A door appears as I tremble cold,
receding portal of fading light.
Frantically clawing to find a hold,
but there's nothing left, and nothing right

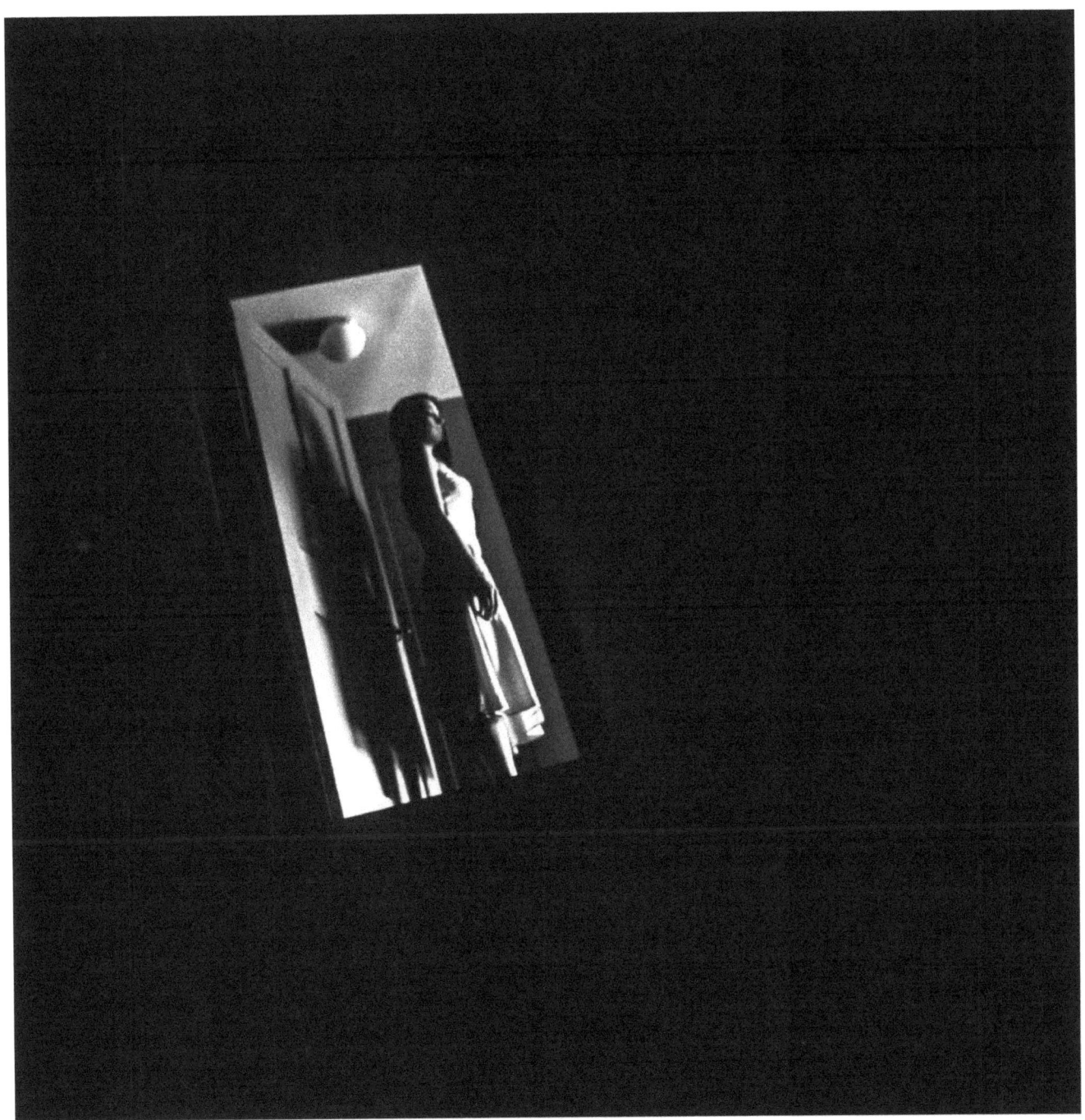

A Little Emptier

Despondent, treading the edges of fear.
Alone, devoid of control.
Who's there to avail me, why am I here?
Want answers, it's taking a toll

Wandering aimlessly—nameless faces
oblivious, no help at all.
Falling down, backing up, of all places
with my back up against the wall

Even when dreaming I'm falling so fast,
then waking last-second, eyes wide
and feeling, after the terror has passed,
a little emptier inside

Insanity

Do it again
Do it again
Do it again

Why can't I get it right?
Am I mad, or does this qualify as practice makes perfect?
Does me worrying about psychosis imply a likelihood that my mind is in fact bent?

Or is it a good thing that I'm conscious of the possibility,
and therefore, more effectual in preventing or subduing it?
And further, if I'm having so much trouble trying to decide
which of those questions is most salient,
is it possible I may already know,
and know the answer as well,
an answer I don't wish to acknowledge?

Then there's always the possibility I'm overthinking things.
Worrying for nothing.
Perhaps it is better to get on with life, with so much to do

Do it again
Do it again
Do it again

Unicorn

Everything is perfect.
Just now, I'm floating
on a baby blue cotton candy cloud.
Someone is playing Enya on a harp nearby
and I'm spooning from a huge crystal bowl of mint chocolate chip

Between mounds of heavenly dotted verdigris,
I grab fistfuls of cloud
and let it go all melty sugary in my mouth
as a golden unicorn sashays gracefully by,
humming along to *Orinoco Flow*

Out of nowhere, a lightning bolt splits the unicorn in two.
His green blood splatters everywhere, dissolving swaths of sweet blue puff.
The music stops, replaced by a chorus of screams.
Covered in my mint dessert (or unicorn blood, which is it?), I begin to sink through.
It grows dark and algid as more thunderbolts crack the sky

I'm falling rapidly now, eyes shut tight.
Hands cupped over my ears to muffle the shrieking.
Praying to wake, apprehensively,
in light of an impending dread for the reality
that will greet me when I do

Hell

Hell is the only word
that quickly comes to mind
as I scan my future
for a positive sign

Where is this fraud called hope?
Tell me how would it feel?
Why does it evade me?
I have no faith it's real

Life has been so painful,
just pain at every turn.
I want to start a fire
and watch the whole thing burn

Among the Ashes

Even when of hope, bereft,
a glint of love refused to die.
Nothing gives like nothing left
where naught but scattered ashes lie

Spectral visions stir the night,
a score of life and loss ago.
Love burned strong and sweet and right.
Idyllic dream that's faded so

Something one can barely see,
an ember's glow amidst the strife.
Scant but steady, guiding me
among the ashes of my life

A Place for Hope

I'll carve a special little niche
safe from the perils of life
where I can make a place for hope.
First, I need to find a knife

A few cuts here, and a few there,
I'll make a nice cubbyhole
where it will not hurt, in between
my dead heart and empty soul

Walls

Efficient compartmentalization,
boxing up pressures and problems like mad.
Tucking away all the unpleasantries,
isolating the happy from the sad

To ignore them is just not sufficient,
imperative they be walled up unseen.
Joys of life are realized unhindered
while riding on pink waves of dopamine

Stoicism in the face of distress,
emotionless gift that keeps on giving.
Then, a burgeoning realization,
this way of life is not really living

Too many walls in every direction
with cryptic boxes stacked too high to see.
I cannot climb out and cannot push through
to wherever I left my empathy

Fear

It comes in without knocking,
rapid and direct.
It's raw and dank and ugly,
not what you expect

And then it really hits you,
awful and grotesque,
it's climbing up inside you,
feeding, monster-esque

It eats your heart, mauls your soul,
still it isn't done.
Crawls into your frightened head,
and with that, it's won

It Just Bleeds

Terrible wound won't heal.
Oozing.
Stitched up and treated with salve,
yet it remains

Interminably

No scar, no promise of a faded reminder.
Instead, it just bleeds.
The pain is constant
but dulled over time.
Probably because
I've learned to ignore it,
at least somewhat.
I can't ignore it forever.
I've tried everything.
Sometimes I stare at it as if I can

will it to repair

But my will has no power here.
So, I'm left with the curious decision—
to cut away the affected area
or change the bandages

Gossamer

Come closer.
A hesitant touch will suffice.
Satiate your curiosity,
or stumble in unwittingly, innocent.
It makes no difference—I'll love you either way

Admire the intriguing, the intricate, strangely beautiful.
Diaphanous, yet strong.
Caress and slowly pull away; or to try...
Perplexed—sticky, it stays, snapping you back.
Then a dose of adrenaline, you're caught and quickly,
frustrated, flailing, afraid.
And I, waiting, longing, heart thumping,
watching, sensing vibrations along the filigree,
feel you struggle, entangled, and I smile.
It only makes me love you more.
My subtle stir catches your eye
and you stop, subdued. Silent.
Gaze locked on mine

I move deliberately, calmly.
Closer.
Your countenance pleads, wondering *why?*
And I respond softly, honestly, still smiling,
because I love you

Sweet Nothings

A Hallmark card,
a knowing smile,
heartfelt devotion in a well-timed text.
Fancy flowers and a bonbon box.
Recognition for that milestone event
Then, back to reality

We'll endure between the mandatories,
the red-letters and festive family fêtes,
the token tributes, the curtain raisers.
And suffer through the blasé Groundhog Day drudgery.
Days of wish you weren't here
so I can do what I want

The circadian affliction of so many things about you that irritate the hell out of me.
All the mind-numbing, excruciating effort that goes into achieving
the absolute minimum acceptable standard of civility.
It's our bulimic rendition of a normal relationship.
We work so hard at it, and it's bearable
because low and behold, there's another Hallmark right around the corner

We'll put aside the thinly veiled disdain for a day.
It'll be all love yous and hugs
and top-shelf chocolates,
and we'll be consoled somehow
by the odd notion
that it's the thought that counts

Vampire

I crave you completely, because it all feels so right.
When we're together, it's perfect. And it really is.
When we're together, the world stops, and it's just us.
But...after all this time, I sense you come at a cost
that is so great, it's as if I'm selling my soul.
At the end, I fear you'll leave me
pale, drained, lifeless

Tempted

Something so sweet to taste, to touch.
All candy to the eye.
To want, to crave, to need so much,
give anything to try

Could treats so good be bad at all?
A hunger oh so strong.
La Dolce Vita is my call;
delicious can't be wrong

Rhapsodic flavors, heaven sent,
ambrosial sugar bliss.
Discretion quickly came and went.
I'm tempted—just a kiss...

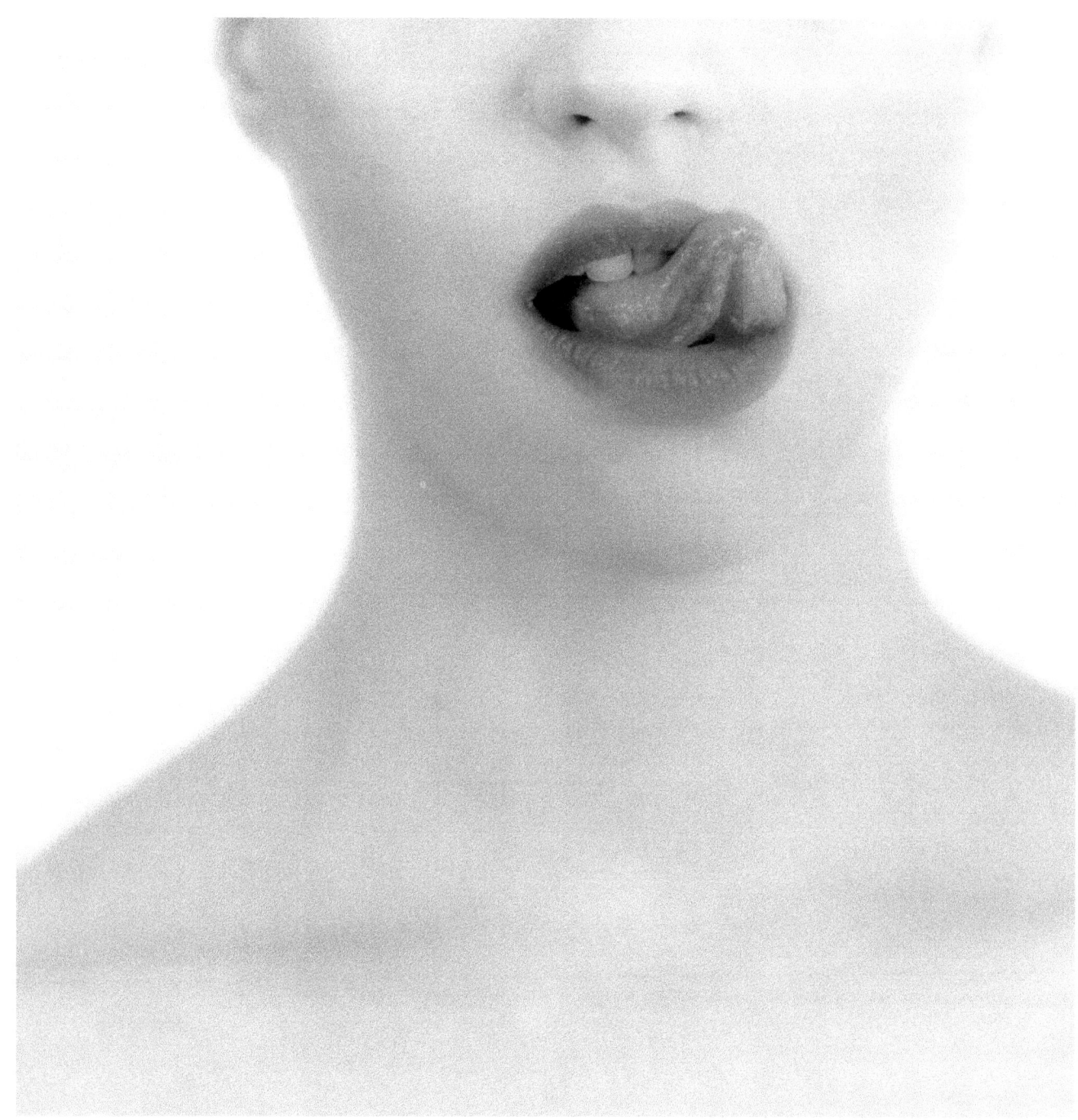

Amoral

What was wrong is just now right,
the right resolves to wrong.
Simply conform base to boss
and you sing a new song

Spin this that way, that to this.
It's quite easy to do.
Discretion is unneeded
where the roadblocks are few

This is right, you say coolly.
And believe it as well.
Now you are blind to the truth
and your sad little hell

Rot in Camouflage

The worst thing you can do is to search for happiness.
You won't ever find it that way.
When you think you have, you find out later
it's something else, an imposter.
All dressed up, pretty and posing

It will avoid the light,
though eventually you will see
sick and decay revealed beneath
an apocryphal cloak.
Your spirit wilts
and you turn to look elsewhere,
only to discover
the next wonderful thing
is also just
rot in camouflage

After a time, you grow weary of searching
and rechannel your spirit
to embrace life as it comes.
Only then does happiness sidle up behind
and tap you on the shoulder

Perdition

Fragments of my existence, parts and pieces
have fallen away and I don't understand
where or how or why.
Parts of something important.
Pieces of something I need

As if some enigmatic hole,
insidious,
scatters the substance of my soul.
I've searched and searched, and on occasion
I note a curious spot,
begin to scratch

Hoping a hole lies beneath.
Wishing and well aware if I dig at it enough,
my wish will come true in a certain sad, wrong way.
The hole, that existential something,
they are never there and I concede, blemished.
Rusty grit beneath my nails

Then I palter.
There's nothing I can do.
And for a time I leave my nails crusted, stained.
A diffident attestation that I may have already lost
everything

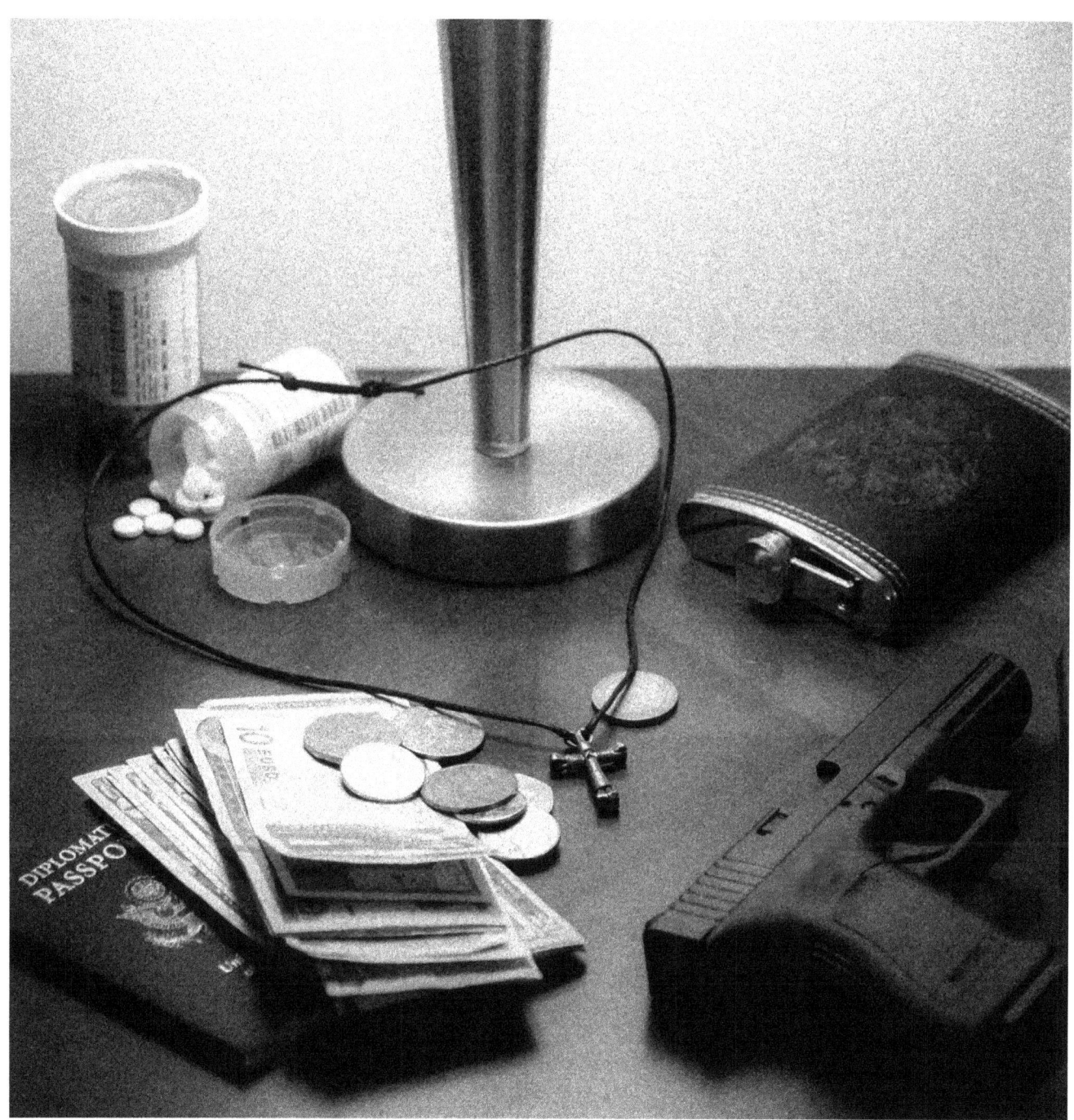

Unfulfilled

Impossible to decide.
Can love bridge such a divide?
Walls between so hard, so high.
How much longer can I try?

One thousand reasons whisper,
with time, you will not miss her.
Love is strong and I, strong-willed.
Could I leave love unfulfilled?

Fitful sleep and restless mind,
what we had I try to find.
Amid the reasons scattered,
I glimpse what really mattered

Hoping, dreaming on I stray
to her smile a world away.
Love unfulfilled, I rise
and a world away, she cries

Apathy

I don't really care.
I'm comfortable right now.
Please don't bother me.
Try to disappear somehow

Blah blah blah, they say.
There's something they really need.
One thing is for sure,
I'm ambivalent, indeed

Looking for concern?
Or some type of emotion?
It better be good,
a real earth-shaking notion

I just don't have time
for all this worthless chatter.
I'm apathetic
because—it doesn't matter

As It Seems

It's obvious
and as it may appear
that everything
is so perfectly clear

A reasoning mind
provides stark clarity,
or so it seems to me

There is no grey,
only black, only white.
Unknowns cannot
disprove what's in plain sight

Perception is
an excuse not to see
that everything's
just as it seems, to me

All Figured Out

I've got it
all figured out

Feeling pretty confident now.
Doesn't matter if others don't agree
'cause I know

There's no twitch of worry or doubt.
I'm not even really thinking about it anymore
'cause I'm totally convinced

I really contemplated it.
Quite a bit, actually

And it made so much sense
that when I was done,
it was like the opposite of an epiphany

It was a no-brainer.
Practically common sense.
It was that easy

Don't even ask me about it
'cause I'm on to the next thing already

Carnation

Why are you like that,
how can you be?
Aromatic origami perfection
confoundingly
unfurled from a tiny green bud

When did you know
you would be so beautiful,
so singular?
Am I the first to extol
how exquisite you are?

I can't help but think
it was your plan
from the start
to make me happy.
Am I the reason, a factor?

Or am I inconsequential to it all—
a random,
forgettable moment
in your delicate,
pastel existence?

Blue

At the moment we met,
right then I suspected.
I saw you once more and was almost certain.
Now it is perfectly clear what an amazing
and beautiful person you are.
My thoughts of you, as sublime as your
deep blue eyes

When we first met,
right then I suspected.
I saw you again and was nearly convinced.
Later it was clear to me what an amazing
and beautiful person you are
My thoughts of you were as sublime as your
deep blue eyes

But you withdrew,
your thoughts obscured.
Your voice guarded,
your gaze averted.
From this new vantage
your eyes are shallow
and more cerulean than blue

Maybe you are amazing and beautiful.
I just can't see it anymore

Cattle

Here comes the train.
A herd of cattle waits to board.
I arrived a little late, but I'll make it.
There goes that same guy once again.
Overweight, shirt tail untucked,
doing his sloppy shuffle run.
Short, quick steps, huffing and puffing
as he scoots his way through the parking lot
with his overstuffed briefcase,
trying to make sure he gets a seat.
How embarrassing

If I ever end up like that—just shoot me

I stand in the aisle, holding on
to a cold stainless silver pipe,
scanning the herd.
Many staring straight ahead, expressionless,
contemplating their empty lives.
Some zoned in on their phones,
tap-tapping likes and emojis.
A few poking at laptops, others asleep.
There's that guy—he got his seat.
He looks satisfied.
Good for him

Narcissism

How thoughtful of you, aren't you nice, just put them over there.
I see you're looking for advice, be that your aim, take care.
You come here with a gift or two just hoping for a thought.
There are countless others like you, and you don't have a shot.
The grandeur and this great success can I alone control
and what you bring cannot impress one solitary soul

Win

Faster, better, smarter—win.
If there's a prize there, I'm all-in.
Golden trophy, it's all mine
before you cross the finish line

Rocket-fueled, rapt ambition.
Fate concedes to my volition.
There is nothing I can't take
wherever there's a win at stake

Bigger, finer, fitter—score.
Each day I'm stronger than before.
Consume the weak, take the haul.
Exceed, subdue and vanquish all

Would That I Were

Wouldn't it be nice if I were funny.
The one who makes everyone laugh, no matter the topic.
That I could, as if by instinct,
create good times from thin air.
To be the life of the party.
Would that I were

Wouldn't it be great if I could solve everyone's problems.
To step in at each moment of turmoil or heartache,
with a few words and gestures, change roadblocks into opportunities,
turn tears into hope.
To be the one everyone leans on.
Would that I were

Wouldn't it be perfect if I could avoid the subjunctive, the hypotheticals.
To be able to fit in and never worry about what others were thinking.
To be free of these vacant, immutable fantasies and released from this ceaseless want of emotional refuge.
To live without fear of a rapid pulse and coursing adrenaline, awkward responses.
Pregnant pauses...*to be normal*.
Would that I were

Evanescence

I know what makes me happy.
Don't try too hard to convince me otherwise.
Sure, I'll listen, and I may even agree with you
for the sake of being polite, however, like I said,
I know

I know because I have proof.
I'm happy right now!
And it's instantaneous.
How can you argue with that?
It's worked every time, every day all year long,
For as long as I can remember.
When life is like this it makes everything
immediately bearable

I need it, don't you see?
With a life like mine, who wouldn't?
Every grim aspect of my existence almost disappears.
Every rut and hole, every wrong turn on this forsaken road to nowhere
for a time, simply vanishes

Chasing the Sun

Caught up in the lure of sunbeams,
slave to mesmerizing light.
There is nothing else that matters,
staring 'til I'm losing sight

Hypnotized by radiant gold,
striking westward constantly.
Praying that it doesn't set, as
horizons shift and taunt me

No time to tire, tend to pain, or
delay for any reason.
Helios beckons ever on,
all the day, every season

Afraid of nightfall closing in,
the lambent god lifts my run.
Flying now on Icarus wings,
cannot help but chase the Sun

Stigma

A sickening twist in the depth of the gut
confirmed my overall impression.
The smell, that look, and his sallow disorder,
such a nasty, diseased obsession

He's a little bit off, almost all the time
and oblivious to the right way.
I'm consumed by disdain being near him
and think hard about what I should say

It'd be better were he to die in the street,
or remanded to life in prison.
Lobotomy might be the only recourse,
an effective, acute incision

He lamented once all he needed was help
as he twisted my gut once again.
We all knew the truth—he's a blight to the world,
a malignant excuse for a man

Really?

That lowborn redneck just cut me in line, TSA agent copped a feel.
Flight is delayed on the departure sign, I've time for an overpriced meal

Wedged between Mr. Sick and Mr. Fat and turbulence for the whole flight.
There's no Wi-Fi, Sorry for that! It's going to be a long night

You know what comes next, my luggage is lost, rental car smells like an ashtray.
Hotel's nearly full, so room's twice the cost; on top of that, it's my birthday

Sloth

I'm so, so tired, want to get out of bed.
What I'd give to be wired, but I lay here instead

I know I need to aspire to some thing.
My 'spirit to be freed', to have 'a song to sing"

Life's there to win—I'd like to, however,
my fourth deadliest sin impedes that endeavor

Too tired to care, I don't know what to say...
I'll get up soon, I swear. Until then, here I lay

Stupid

Stupid noises, I can't sleep,
stupid counting stupid sheep.
Stupid breakfast, I can't eat,
stupid eggs with stupid meat.
Stupid drivers, stupid roads,
stupid trucks with stupid loads.
Stupid work I hate my job,
stupid Amy, stupid Bob.
Stupid people in my face,
stupid people everyplace.
Stupid luck that just won't last,
stupid future, stupid past

The Insanity of It All

All the day-to-day crazy, it leaves me climbing up a wall.
The rude, the mean, the lazy—the insanity of it all

It takes all I can muster to raise the proverbial bar,
to cut through all the bluster, see things for what they truly are

Reach down deep and draw a line, continue thinking, walking tall.
The problem's theirs, never mine—the insanity of it all

Quiet

I want it quiet.
No talking, no rustling, no clinking, no sound.
The beauty of silence, in all its nothingness, emptiness, loneliness,
allows me to think

There is a gravity about it, a certain importance I cannot quite convey.
Yet it is there, amidst the nothing,
throughout the empty,
in the lonely

Listen

Life begins with a whisper, a laugh, a smile, a touch.
With care it grows into something wonderful.
Life is love. I want so to live

Living is so misunderstood—too often correlated with eating,
drinking, using, working, earning, accumulating...
It's no wonder we are so messed up

Even the happiest fall prey to the plastic, the vacuous virtual,
and some little voice keeps whispering to us, *there's something wrong here.*
Listen

Final Act

As I take the stage, I can just see the signs,
veiled memories of happily ever after.
With some effort, I listen between the lines
of this sad tragedy, and I can hear laughter

There's a trace of merry in this pantomime,
enough to leave my waning sanity intact.
It is something I crave almost all the time.
To take advantage of it, I will have to act

I'm grasping for some sense of alacrity
and the compulsion to perform in a broad way
before life's random curtain call retires me
from this tired satire, this comically absurd play

Optimism

It's difficult not to focus on the void.
Moreover, and complicating things,
is the common misunderstanding
that we are bound to the glass at hand

It might help to consider that things are infinitely better at half,
having begun at empty,
or that, even having started at full,
half is still halfway there

But even at the best of times, the understanding
that you'll never be able to fill it more than full
leaves potential for a positive outlook somewhat fettered.
Think outside the glass

Mine is never empty.
And how full it is depends on the success I have
with the continuous effort I put
into finding a source to replenish it

Mine is also never completely full.
I make sure of it.
When it looks like it's getting there,
I trade in for a bigger glass

Honey

Buzz, buzz, buzz...
Busy, busy, beautiful bees.
Not a care, save the pollen and the pupae.
And the queen of course

Workers work all day long,
collecting, protecting, feeding.
And drones drone—fatherless, yet fathers.
Altogether, a sweet arrangement

Gaia

An aura of radiant energy
envelops her form as she goes.
The Sun and the Moon look on jealously
as she strikes a celestial pose

The flora nearby are drawn to her muse
and fauna assemble in tow.
Seraphic empress of all she imbues
with life and ethereal glow

Alive

I harbor an unbridled ardor of life.
An impassioned love for living.
Not for being, for existence.
Rather, a zeal for the Earth's entire spectrum
of possibilities and experiences to choose from and to do.
And to choose all the right ones

Or at least, the right ones most of the time.
And with recognition that choosing to do nothing,
or even the next best thing, because of apprehension or fear
is a coward's failure—a craven dereliction.
It is a love of life so strong, there is no consideration
for casual worry or petty irritants

Those temporary inconveniences,
the lulls and lows between countless majestic peaks
are awash with the whitewater thrill of it all
and overcome by the promise of a next summit.
And then to climb.
Because I can

Because it's there, because it's daunting.
Because I know how truly alive I will be at the pinnacle.
To be one with the resplendent grandeur of nature,
at times so stunning and so vast
the only way to begin to comprehend it
is to have been there

In the Ascent

Scaling a formidable mountainside,
clarity awaits at the top.
Every footfall lucidity accrues.
Arduous task, yet mustn't stop

Somehow more resilient with altitude.
The Earth's beauty is in full view.
Comprehending more the more we behold,
the horizon constantly new

Fewer now by my side as I ascend.
Some turned back; sadly, others fell.
Those still at it are as keen as I am
to summit strongly, I can tell

Countless ridgelines mistaken for the crest,
but we harbor no discontent.
The climb an evolving destiny now
and the reward, in the ascent

Real

I felt cheated when you got in the car.
All the pleasantries and mandatory talk got in the way.
What I wanted to say had to wait and oh God, the traffic
But at least one genuine thing came out of it,
when I played that song I like, and you liked it too.
Or at least you said you did

But my friend with problems kept calling,
even after we arrived, to meet the others.
And there were formalities,
with folks brainstorming and talking all around,
serious and businesslike
Cheated again, why can't we just talk?
And with you sitting there
acting ten years older than you look,
all I could do was just smile

Again in the car with the traffic,
you bent the pages of my book,
showing me where to read
and what was best.
That was real.
That was what I wanted

True Love

So hard to describe how I know that it's true,
I don't quite know where to begin.
Like conveying the sight of a sunrise
to someone who's always slept in

I know that it's true without any doubt,
I see it in every way.
She joins me in sleep, greets me each morning,
and stays with me all through the day

So beautiful I cannot help but stare,
inspires without having to try.
Beaming and bright, her warmth melts my heart,
and her spirit lights up my sky

We Were There

Dreams of you smiling, when we were there.
The sweet taste of your skin, sun on your hair.
Reposed on a mountain, searching the sky,
we wondered together, love or goodbye

Ephemeral moments, vibrant and real.
Yet, so far away now, I cannot feel.
Dreams my only refuge, lost reverie.
We were there, together—you, love, and me

With You

How will we know, how will it be? One if by land, two if by sea?
Where will we go, how to construe?
Somehow it doesn't matter, as long as it's how and where with you

When to know the moment is nigh? Epiphany, or sign in the sky?
When we get there, what will we do?
Somehow it's not important, as long as it's when and what with you

Why you—soul, body, mind and voice? Love and passion, fate or choice?
Made for each other, through and through?
Somehow it is all of these, as long as life lasts, why I'm with you

Sinfonietta

A constant patter.
No, a soft chorus.
Calming.
Billions of diminutive droplets punctuated by unfamiliar chirps.
Beautiful, are they frogs?

Moist air, thick.
Resonant with the melodic trills of largish alien bugs
shrouded by impossibly large, glistening leaves.
An exotic bird warbles rhythmically.
I see him, neon and still

Solo,

watching me with one eye.
Everything here seems like nowhere else, ever,
to be playing together.
A cappella.
A harmonious arrangement

In the distance, a tree falls.
The bird darts away.
Trills and chirps fall off,
the rain fades

Outro

Love Song

From there, on to eternity,
rare palette of notes in my mind.
A herald of love's prophecy
that's there to hear, yet hard to find

Sustained by a refrain so strong,
the melody too real to fade.
A whispered, emotional song,
every hour and day, always played

A distant place not long ago,
born of love, a symphony there.
Yearning for a sweet crescendo,
in time, I pray, somehow, somewhere

Note from the Heart

A little note,
for your pocket.
You can read it from time to time
and it will help you feel

Every waking moment
your angel's heart beats in mine.
Is it enough that you feel it too?
Do you hear it?

It is strong enough, if I listen,
to bend time, shape destiny.
The fates pay deference to the power of our love.
Our disparate paths converge, I feel it

Keep this note in your pocket, my angel.
It will remind you of the passion in my heart for yours.
Hear it, feel it beating stronger
as we journey closer

Flight

I'm flying.
Direction doesn't matter,
no particular destination in mind.
It's all about how I'm getting there

When I land is immaterial.
And if I never do, no worry.
Gravity has become a foreign concept,
a law that no longer pertains, for the most part, to me

My empyrean journey takes me wherever the wind blows,
or cloud to cloud on a lightning flash.
Aloft amidst the Northern Lights and majestic starfield nights.
A grand mercurial adventure, nonpareil

If you could see what I've seen,
feel as I feel soaring zoetic above it all,
euphorically embracing the heavens...
And all the while, knowing *there's so much more*

Ever

It felt like a lifetime since I'd seen you.
I waited with such anticipation,
staring hard through the crowd as if I knew
where you'd appear, all glow and elation

in a red dress with a bounce in your gait.
You'd be smiling a wide, warm, heart-deep smile.
Driven by passion and guided by fate,
you'll move confidently with grace and style

striding faster as your heart is racing.
We then fall into each other until,
lip to lip, eye to eye, we're embracing
each other oh so tightly, nothing will

ever pull us apart again. *Ever*

Pieces of Me

He's almost as tall as me now, it seemed to happen overnight.
His voice, deeper and expressing cogent, independent thoughts.
Thoughts I engendered.
Some that have evolved into his own discriminating convictions and dreams.
I catch myself wondering if I may soon begin to learn from him

She's more and more just like her mom,
with a blithely unique, emotive personality,
an ethereal love of nature and life that rivals most.
A love we've shared from day one.
When I gaze into her eyes, I don't need to try too hard to see pieces of me in there

I feel as if it were yesterday both were so dependent, so spiritually attached.
Veritable extensions of my soul.
But now they stray, testing the boundaries of adolescence.
Venturing beyond the protective barriers I so carefully constructed.
And as they go, so go
certain chimeric fragments of my existence

I'm hesitant to let them slip away, but know I must.
Little by little.
And I know as well I will somehow remain whole,
as long as they come back to me
from time to time

Beauty's Smile

A sorrow I feel, for beauty in distress.
Delicate, bent and weeping.
Assailed by

hurt

I cannot forgive even nature
when one so fair
lies beholden to her darker purpose

This indiscriminate torment cannot thrive.
My focused hope sees it drawn out and carried away,
harmlessly, by the next gentle wind

Rise early with the Sun.
Tomorrow brings new strength, with my sorrow but a memory
and my heart warm at the return of beauty's smile

Little Bunny

Little bunny is what he calls her when they're together.
When he wants her to know
she is loved

No one else can have this name.
It's reserved for her alone,
as silly as it may seem to others

He's careful even not to say 'little' or 'bunny'
when referring to other people or things if she is near.
Even when unpaired, those words are sort of hers, by extension

It's an intimately special thing.
No other will ever fully understand.
Even when they think they do, they'll not have it quite right

And that's fine,
he doesn't want them to,
because it's just for her

Gratitude

I find it all too easy to overlook the good things.
I suppose this is common,
but I don't wish to be common
I remind myself...

I'm grateful for your smile,
with the way your eyes sparkle when you do,
telling me it's from the heart

For the cool clean air on a mountaintop
where one can see for miles
and realize how small we really are

I'm grateful for your laugh, whether in jest or joy.
You remind me of the fullness of life and invite me to join in.
For the opportunity to start each new day with a sunrise and a purpose

I'm grateful for the little things you do for me.
Not to show me you love me,
rather, *because* you love me

I'm grateful for so much, too much to list here.
But most of all, I'm grateful for you
and I thank God for every living moment
I've had the chance to love you back

Φ

If you believe you have found yourself, keep searching.

You are deeper than you think.

Phi is the mathematical symbol for the Golden Ratio, an irrational number. Its origin is generally attributed to Phidias, a 5th century BC Greek sculptor and mathematician who studied Phi and incorporated the ratio into his work on the Parthenon and Olympus. In the 12th century, Leonardo Fibonacci wrote a simple numerical sequence that is the foundation for the mathematical relationship of Phi. Beginning with zero and one, each new number in the sequence is simply the sum of the two before it. Zero and one combine to one, one and one combine to two, two and one to three, three and two to five, and so on. The ratio of each number in the series to the one before it converges on Phi as you move towards infinity.

The Golden Ratio is commonly found in nature, with a tendency toward beauty and perfection. For example, the ratio is expressed in the shape of a nautilus shell, in the way a growing fern unfurls, and in the unique family tree of a honeybee colony.

In order to achieve sustained spiritual growth and serenity, you must first accept that it is your thoughts that make you who you are. You can then continuously strive, in harmony with others, for improvement and understanding of self by comprehending and amending what and how you think. With this ability you will achieve a deeper and more accurate understanding of the world and of your place in it, and you will experience increased joy and contentment. Just as the Golden Ratio is only perfect at infinity, you will never attain states of perfect enlightenment and happiness—you can only attempt to approach them, day by day.

Reflect on your thoughts, understand and learn from who you were yesterday. Then add that knowledge to who you are today. In this manner, you will be a more knowledgeable and spiritual person tomorrow.

Then do it again tomorrow. And the next day...

Acknowledgements

Anna Apostolova: *her*

Roman Katok: *him*

Sweet Little Sofia: *child*

Jim Rohn, an acclaimed personal development author and speaker, famously wrote, *"It is the set of the sails, not the direction of the wind that determines which way we will go."* I admire this thought for its emphasis on taking purposeful action now for the future (something *Raw Thoughts* prompts us to do), and because of the word "we." What we can achieve together is, more often than not, much greater than what one can accomplish alone.

In 2015 I had just begun arranging the stockpile of poems I had penned, and realized they were connected, a loosely coherent amalgam. There were thematic elements across various works that appeared to tell parts of a story. The story was vague but visceral; terrible and beautiful; haunting, hopeful, and joyful. And it was *real*. But there was something missing—I wanted to add an artistic element that was equally compelling and indelibly symbiotic with the writing—to make it whole, and in a manner where the whole was greater than the sum of its parts.

Any assumption that I would be successful in thanking everyone who had an impact in the creation of this book would be shortsighted—there were so many. That said, there are a few who made significant contributions. To start, *Raw Thoughts* would have been so much less without the singular photographic talent of Scott Hussey. Friends since boyhood, Scott and I spent a year developing and refining the photography concepts and planning production. It was Scott's suggestion that we use vintage cameras and film (vice digital) for the photography—an artistic decision that added a dimension of genuineness; film photography somehow looks and feels more real—deeper, than digital. The results were sublime.

I changed the name of the book a couple times, and eventually settled on the simple, self-descriptive title '*Raw Thoughts.*' I then incorporated the Golden Ratio as an underlying philosophy, which underpins the themes of mindfulness and positive psychology throughout the book. The precept that we will become more complete and better people each day in the examination, assessment, and improvement of our thinking fit closely with the spiritual interpretation of the Golden Ratio. Serendipitously, Scott incorporates the mathematical curve of the Ratio into his approach to photography as well, something I wasn't aware of until I brought the idea to him.

As I began to seek advice and unofficial reviews from close friends and colleagues, I found that people related to the book. The supposition that *what and how we think is who we really are* is not a new one. However, in *Raw Thoughts* I believed we created something that embodied such an intellection in a truly unique and inspirational way.

The right people continued to emerge as we moved forward. Anna Apostolova was an accomplished model from Ukraine who had settled in Massachusetts. She was attracted to the project in part because her mother is a successful writer and poet. Roman Katok, our male model, travelled from Pennsylvania to participate in one of the two (very long) photo shoots in various locations across New Hampshire and Vermont. Thank you so much Roman and Anna for your collaboration.

Michelle Baker, a friend I'd worked with on a local nonprofit, helped me extensively with marketing research and publication submission preparation. She also introduced me to Sheryl Nelms. Sheryl is a prolific poet from Texas with (many) thousands of published works. Sheryl reviewed *Raw Thoughts* at different stages of completion. Her advice and commentary were helpful in guiding the evolution of a loosely connected assemblage of poems and photos into a compelling and mindful fusion of poetic and photographic art.

There were others involved in the production of the photography. Deb Gadreau from Salon Exodus and Victoria McIntosh from Moda Suo Studios provided many hours of on-site hair and makeup artistry for our photo shoots. Studio One in Keene, NH did hair and makeup for Anna as well. Drue Seksinsky, a skilled and experienced rock climber, provided gear, guidance, and safety instruction for one of our riskier shots. And special thanks go out to my sister, Anna, for her support in allowing my angelic niece Sofia to be part of the project.

In writing this, I had to consider where this all came from—ostensibly, my head. But it didn't all start in there. What and how we think may be the best representation of our true self, but that thinking was influenced heavily along the way, sometimes rightly, sometimes wrongly. In the end, we are influenced most by a close circle of family, friends, and colleagues. Thank you all.

First Publications

This list includes credits for poems published previously in literary journals and magazines. In most cases, original poems were adapted for the Second Edition of *Raw Thoughts*.

Rot in Camouflage, Real—March 5, 2018, Anapest Journal

Sinfonietta, Love Song, Note from The Heart (Poem and Photo)—March 24, 2018, Remembered Arts Journal

Stigma—April 4, 2018, Pamplemousse

Listen—April 25, 2018, Into the Void Magazine

Reflection, Stellar—May 24, 2018, Flumes Literary Journal

Sweet Nothings—June 8, 2018, Sheila-Na-Gig Online

Flight (Poem and Photo)—August 25, 2018, Remembered Arts Journal

Optimism—October 2, 2018, Anapest Journal

Subsistence of Loss (Photo)— February 15, 2018, Runner Up, Raw Art Review Art of Storm and Urge Contest, The Raw Art Review

Skeletons (Photo)—December 15, 2018, The Raw Art Review

A Place for Hope (Poem and Photo)—December 15, 2018, Remembered Arts Journal

Unicorn—January 1, 2019, Coffin Bell Journal

About the Author

JOHN CASEY is a Pushcart Prize-nominated poet and novelist from New Hampshire with a Master of Arts from Florida State University. He authored the First Edition of *Raw Thoughts: A mindful Fusion of Poetic and Photographic Art* in 2019, which was nominated for the Griffin Poetry Prize and National Book Award. The Second Edition of *Raw Thoughts* and *Meridian: A Raw Thoughts Book* followed in 2021. His poetry has been published internationally in numerous literary journals and magazines. Casey authored *Devolution* in 2019 as well, book one of The Devolution Trilogy. *Evolution*, book two, and *Revelation* round out the psychological spy thriller series. A Veteran combat tactical airlift and developmental test pilot, Casey also served as a diplomat and international affairs strategist at U.S. embassies in Germany and Ethiopia, the Pentagon, and elsewhere. He is passionate about fitness, nature, and the human spirit and inspired by the incredible spectrum of people, places, and cultures he has experienced in life.

www.ingramcontent.com/pod-product-compliance
Lightning Source LLC
Chambersburg PA
CBHW051257110526
44589CB00025B/2858